Z-105
IVAN THE TERRIBLE

FRONT ENDPAPER: Celebration of Russia's victory over Tatar invaders.
BACK ENDPAPER: The scene of Anastasia's death.

Photography by Vladimir Pchalkin
Captions by Dr. Herbert R. Axelrod

Cover: Natalya Bessmertnova
and Irek Mukhamedov.

IVAN THE TERRIBLE

Yuri Grigorovich in the Bolshoi.

THE AUTHORIZED BOLSHOI BALLET BOOK OF

IVAN THE TERRIBLE

By Yuri Grigorovich and Alexander Demidov

Translated from the Russian by N. Levcoeva

Published and distributed throughout the world by T.F.H. Publications, Inc.

Published through the cooperation
of VAAP Copyright Agency of the Soviet Union.

Distributed in the UNITED STATES by T.F.H. Publications, Inc., One T.F.H. Plaza, Neptune City, NJ 07753; in CANADA to the Book Trade by Macmillan of Canada (A Division of Canada Publishing Corporation), 164 Commander Boulevard, Agincourt, Ontario M1S 3C7; in ENGLAND by T.F.H. Publications Limited, Cliveden House/Priors Way/Bray, Maidenhead, Berkshire SL6 2HP, England; in AUSTRALIA AND THE SOUTH PACIFIC by T.F.H. (Australia) Pty. Ltd., Box 149, Brookvale 2100 N.S.W., Australia; in NEW ZEALAND by Ross Haines & Son, Ltd., 18 Monmouth Street, Grey Lynn, Auckland 2, New Zealand; in SINGAPORE AND MALAYSIA by MPH Distributors (S) Pte., Ltd., 601 Sims Drive, #03/07/21, Singapore 1438; in the PHILIPPINES by Bio-Research, 5 Lippay Street, San Lorenzo Village, Makati Rizal; in SOUTH AFRICA by Multipet Pty. Ltd., 30 Turners Avenue, Durban 4001. Published by T.F.H. Publications, Inc. Manufactured in the United States of America by T.F.H. Publications, Inc.

CONTENTS

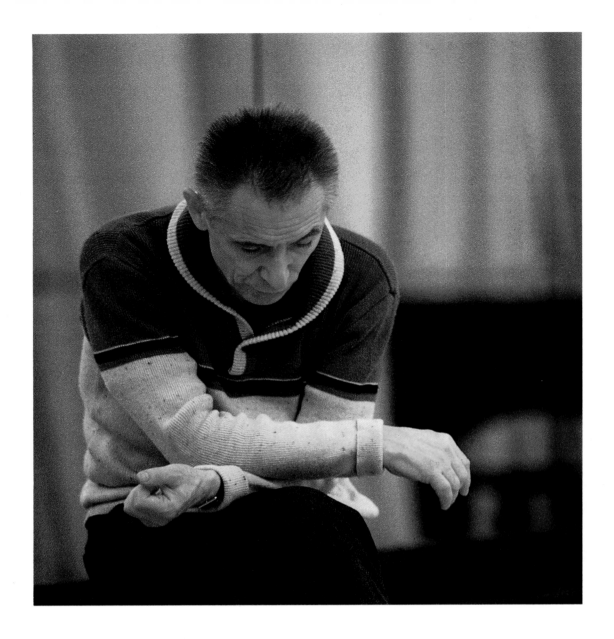

Yuri Grigorovich: Ballet for me is theatre, first and foremost. But still it is a special type of theatre which does not imitate drama. It has its own unique language based on classical technique. In *Ivan the Terrible* I wanted to prove the fertile creative potential of the classical ballet. This production played an important role in the company's progress.

The Bolshoi is in a way the Academy of ballet which preserves the best from its past experience. But Bolshoi is not a museum theatre. Therefore respect for traditions means not only mastering the heritage but also permanent development of the genre and search for new ways. This is what I tried to do in *Ivan the Terrible*—it was my way to create a new form of a contemporary ballet which has both classical background and contemporary expressive means and which gives us the feeling of the present-day world that surrounds us.

IVAN THE TERRIBLE

A two-act ballet.
Music by Sergei Prokofiev
Score by M. Chulaki
Libretto by Yuri Grigorovich

Produced by Yuri Grigorovich in 1976.

In order to understand the story of IVAN THE TERRIBLE, and the meaning of the various dances and scenes, begin reading the captions to the photographs starting on page 49. A synopsis of the ballet is on p. 48

SUPPLEMENTARY INFORMATION
ABOUT THE COLOR PHOTOGRAPHS

The exterior of the Bolshoi Hall in Moscow.

Sergei Prokofiev 1891-1953.

Preface

It was extremely interesting and exciting work. Work that aroused a number of sudden and knotty problems. That was due to the fact that our ballet theatre had hardly been interested before in plots from Russian history. And such productions rarely attracted choreographers. That was why the work at *Ivan the Terrible* was a real opportunity and gave me the feeling of discovery.

In the Soviet art of the 70's, a great interest in the history and culture of Old Russia was developed. Thus, the ballet theatre in answer to the demands of the times was looking for broader contacts with the audience.

It could hardly keep apart from the main streams in art—history itself, its tendencies and the main stages in the development of the Russian State—all that was a major concern for artists who wanted to portray it by new artistic means.

Our ballet theatre as well came to review its potential and then made itself familiar with new subjects that departed from the traditional ballet themes. And historical plots would have to occupy a special position.

For a long time I was thrilled with the idea of creating a ballet based on Russian history. And before the conception of *Ivan the Terrible* came to my mind I had been working with different librettos. Still the task seemed so difficult to me that I could not foresee its realization. It was hard to both find the plot and to define the contemporary means for portraying the events and the characters of the remote past. But the main difficulty was to find appropriate music.

As a result I've chosen the music by Sergei Prokofiev, a great composer of the 20th century, a composer of the national spirit, a composer with a deep sense of history.

Ivan the Terrible was not just based on Prokofiev's music. It was inspired by all his heritage, for the great Soviet artist had defined different trends in the Soviet ballet theatre. The fact that the ballet dedicated to Russian history was staged to Prokofiev's music seems to me symbolic and justified.

Yuri Grigorovich

Author's note

Ivan the Terrible is a new and original work. That's why in this book can be found all the stages of its creation: beginning from the idea to its realization.

Five years of research

Grigorovich had never worked at any of his productions for as long a time as he worked at this one. Initially the idea to create a ballet about Ivan the Terrible came to him in January 1970. The première took place five years later—in the winter of 1976. Meanwhile Grigorovich changed the libretto and the score and made the general idea of the work more precise. The final conception was evolving slowly. Still, there were moments when he was about to give everything up.

Why was it so? What stood in his way and what troubled him? Why did it take him so long to finish the work?

Chapter 1
Origin of the Idea

In December 1969, when *Swan Lake* was being revived, Grigorovich was thinking over a plot for a new ballet. Quite different works interested him at that time: Gogol's *Petersburg Stories*, Dostoevsky's *Idiot*, Bulgakov's newly published sensational *Master and Margaret* and Arbuzov's contemporary play *The Irkutsk Story*, the latter found its realization in the ballet *Angara* (staged in 1976).

At that very time Grigorovich was far from thinking of any plot based on Russian history and connected with Ivan the Terrible. But two weeks after the première of *Swan Lake*, the idea of a ballet centered around Ivan the Terrible and his epoch first came to the choreographer's mind.

A well-known Leningrad conductor, N. Stassevich, suggested creating a ballet to Prokofiev's music for Eisenstein's film *Ivan the Terrible*. There were a number of musical pieces arranged by Stassevich in the form of an oratorio that included both symphonic and vocal fragments supplied with a commentary. Thus, Stassevich gave Prokofiev's music a new life, and it was excellent stuff from which to make a ballet production.

At first Grigorovich accepted the idea with little enthusiasm. But once he familiarized himself with the oratorio compiled by Stassevich he changed his mind. Musical fragments put together and arranged into a certain composition were brilliantly played by the orchestra conducted by Stassevich and they attracted Grigorovich's attention by the theatricality and intensity of emotion. "I realized at once that it was music deserving great performance," the choreographer says today.

At the same time he had a rather vague idea about the plot of the ballet to this music. "I wasn't even sure whether this production would be about Ivan the Terrible. I mean, not only about his life," says Grigorovich. "The music offered broad associations. It suggested either the form of a ballet-chronicle or a mosaic picture from Russian history, etc., etc."

Stassevich's idea "worked." He was acquainted with Grigorovich's productions staged in Leningrad and he was sure his suggestion would hit the mark. Firstly, Grigorovich began his career with Prokofiev's ballet, *The Stone Flower*, that both brought success to the young choreographer and revealed his knowledge of Russian folklore and the Russian national character. Secondly, in *Legend of Love* and *Spartacus*, Grigorovich demonstrated his amazing skills in creating large-scale mass scenes required by the very character of the ballet *Ivan the Terrible*. Thirdly, Prokofiev's music to Eisenstein's film was full of real dramatism and passion and conflicts which Grigorovich valued highly in ballet theatre. Furthermore, Stassevich's oratorio outlined the possible contrasts of action: fast changes of epic and intimate scenes, cruel, bloody, melodramatic, ritual, and lyrical fragments, that fitted Grigorovich's tastes.

Thus, he made his choice. "At that moment nothing but music was leading me," says Grigorovich.

Situation

The years 1968–69 were marked by great triumphs in Grigorovich's career, though they brought him some troubles and presented a number of new problems related to his position as the Bolshoi Ballet's artistic director.

1968 was his third season at the Bolshoi. This was the period of acquaintance with a large company, with its mixed esthetically heterogeneous repertoire. Grigorovich came to a company that had gone through hard times caused by the general crisis of the main trend the Soviet ballet had experienced for the previous 25 years.

In Soviet criticism this trend is called "ballet-drama." It is known for the overuse of conventional details to the detriment of poetic images in dance and for the replacement of the complex choreographic language by naturalistic pantomime. Apologists of this trend proclaimed the idea of converting ballet into realistic drama built according to the laws of the "spoken" theatre. They failed to understand that each art form had its own unique and individual nature.

No doubt this trend had its own achievements: ballet-drama productions were distinguished by a deep sense of dramaturgy; their plots were based on Russian and world classical literature, and the role of a dancer-actor—the creator of true and vital images—became more significant.

But it became evident that at the same time there was a lack of dancing, poetry and imagery. Artistry was substituted by naturalism and the attempt to overcome this lessening by using stage effects led to superficial, pompous, gala productions.

The crisis in the ballet theatre of 40s–50s had a harmful effect on the leading Soviet company—the Bolshoi Ballet. In spite of the fact that the company had a good number of brilliant dancers, its life was dull and monotonous. And though there were about 20 ballets in the company's repertoire, the artistic potential of the dancers wasn't completely revealed.

Grigorovich, already known as a young and talented choreographer, an artist full of energy and plans, was accepted with enthusiasm by the company. The dancers craved real work and the whole company needed an artistic success that would restore its self-confidence and firm belief in the future.

The desired success was brought by the first ballets Grigorovich staged at the Bolshoi: *The Legend of Love* appeared in 1965 and *Nutcracker* a year later. In these two productions both great masters and young dancers had the opportunity to demonstrate their talents in full. The corps-de-ballet which constitutes the basis of any large company received an utterly new function when, from a faceless mass of extras, it became an equal participant in the performance. For Grigorovich it was an important victory both artistic and tactical. Corps-de-ballet dancers are like musicians in an orchestra who can reject a conductor and thus make his life rather complicated. Grigorovich was looking for the support of the corps-de-ballet without infringing on the stars' interests.

The success of his productions staged in Moscow resulted in the consolidation of the company. And this was even more important for the choreographer as he had many "outside" opponents. Choreographers of the "ballet-drama" trend didn't want Grigorovich to be head of the leading ballet company. The stronger his position within the company was, the weaker were his opponents.

Nevertheless the success of *The Legend of Love* and *Nutcracker* couldn't solve all the problems. There was a demand for greater, really immense success which could have an unprecedented public response. The poetic and intimate *Nutcracker*, though a masterpiece, could not serve the purpose, and *The Legend of Love*—one of the best among Grigorovich's ballets—was rather exotic and elite. *Nutcracker* used to be considered a ballet for children. The ancient Oriental tale of *The Legend of Love* was not a popular one and the name of the young composer, A. Melikov, was quite unknown.

In the season of 1967–68 Grigorovich began his work on *Spartacus* by A. Khachaturian, a composer who enjoyed wide popularity at that time. Among the heroes of the past, Spartacus as the leader of the rebellious gladiators, was very close to new Soviet Russia, to its ideas and its concept of art with what it called "positive character," ready to give up his life in the name of world justice.

There were a number of *Spartacus* productions before Grigorovich: in Leningrad (1956) and later in Moscow and other cities of the Soviet Union. They were quite different but none of them enjoyed real success. Nevertheless, the ballet always aroused public interest due to its exciting music and plot.

No doubt Grigorovich found his own approach to *Spartacus*. The ballet had a special meaning for the choreographer, for his artistic credo.

The première of *Spartacus* took place in 1968 and the production enjoyed enormous success. It was a triumph that announced the beginning of a new era in Soviet ballet art.

Spartacus won worldwide recognition too. During the London tour of the Bolshoi in Autumn 1969 it was a great success as none of the Russian ballets had ever been before.

Very enthusiastic about the success of *Spartacus* Grigorovich began his new work. But at about the same time some difficulties caused by his version of *Swan Lake* arose.

The choreographer was reproached for a wrong interpretation of Russian classics. That encouraged his former opponents. Furthermore, there were some members of the company who didn't accept his conception of *Swan Lake*. Thus, there was stormy indignation because the national divertissement dances had been transformed into classical ones which were now performed by classical dancers, not by character dancers. Similar changes were made by Grigorovich in *The Sleeping Beauty* and *Nutcracker*. It gave the opponents the reason to accuse him of renouncing the approach specially taught at ballet schools.

Also, instead of a light and beautiful fairy tale with a happy ending, Grigorovich suggested a tragic and moving story with Odetta's death at the finale. For the London tour the Bolshoi chose the old version.

In 1970 Grigorovich was awarded the Lenin Prize for *Spartacus*. That marked the official and public recognition of his work, though he still had a lot of problems.

At the beginning of 1970 Grigorovich entered a new period of his career.

The previous period when he had familiarized himself with the company and its repertoire, when he had enjoyed first successes and happy days with the company, was over.

What would be next? The alliance between Grigorovich and the company in *Spartacus* made the project of long joint work quite real. But contrasting views on *Swan Lake* hinted at future problems.

As the leader of the Bolshoi Ballet, Grigorovich had to take more global and general tasks connected with the expansion of his own style, new principles of management, new repertoire policy, bringing up new generations of dancers.

Moreover, he had to create a new Bolshoi Ballet. The Bolshoi Ballet of Yuri Grigorovich. That's why the choice of a story for the production to follow *Swan Lake* had a special meaning for the choreographer.

Polemics on the subject

The 16th century Russian tsar Ivan Vassilyevich belonged to the Uld Rurik House. He ascended to the throne as Ivan IV. Soon people nicknamed him Ivan the Terrible. With time this came to be his surname. In Russian history and scholarly works Ivan IV is still frequently called Ivan the Terrible.

The origin of this appellation is unknown. There exist different legends, but they could have appeared and spread after the tsar had been given his new name. Some legends ascribe it to a terrible thunderstorm that broke out in Moscow when the tsar was born. Others mention various omens and prophecies that preceded the birth of a new tsar who would terrify the Moscow State. In other sources the origin of the nickname is more prosaic and related to the political activities of the tsar marked with mass repressions of opponents, mainly boyars.

It is not that important, however, when and why the nickname came into being. It might have been the tsar himself as he loved precise, expressive, and striking epithets. The point is that the word *terrible* is the most accurate one to characterize his personality and his rule, and even his aspirations and goals. He, tsar Ivan IV, had to be terrible at a time when Russia was facing a crisis in both economy and politics. The country was devastated and ruined by the Mongolian yoke, and it was divided into numerous feudal principalities. He had to be *terrible* for external and internal enemies, even for close people and his own family, as he was the embodiment of the very spirit of the times—the times of great reforms aimed at the formation of a united Russian State, one of the biggest and influential powers in Europe. That was the covert aspiration that motivated the rule of Ivan the Terrible. He wanted to change the historical destiny of Russia and to overcome its backwardness.

Ivan the Terrible, his personality, his epoch and his rule that lasted for half a century, had different interpretations at different periods of time.

Why do historians still show lively interest in Ivan IV and join the old polemics with new arguments?

It is obvious that in the succession of Russia's rulers, Ivan the Terrible occupies a special place. Although he failed to achieve all his goals in foreign policy and to solve the economic problems Russia faced at that time, he was the founder of the ideology of Russian statehood and of the principles of the corresponding totalitarian political regime. To some extent all Russian autocrats were successors of Ivan IV and they further developed his ideological programme. Ivan the Terrible was a rare statesman—he was a publicist-tsar, an ideologist-tsar. This explains interest of historians in Ivan IV and his times, as they turned to the sources of social reality and tried to find the links between the past and the present, to formulate their attitude towards history where the figure of Ivan IV was one of the most important ones.

There exist numerous scholarly works related to Ivan the Terrible and his rule, though different and rather controversial points of view can be found therein. The debates centered around the question as to what extent the cruelty of Ivan the Terrible was justified and the means he had chosen to gain autocratic power were legitimate.

Ivan the Terrible would find both supporters and opponents, ardent advocates and irreconcilable enemies. Some people presented him as a criminal and villain. Others consider him a wise and clever politician whose cruelty was nothing but a myth. It is rather curious that every author could make reference to facts which would prove this or that argument and everyone would be right to some extent. It is still more curious that nearly all of the opponents would attempt to explain the phenomenon of Ivan the Terrible proceeding not from the principles of scientific analysis, but rather from the prevailing tastes of their own time, from its ideological and political goals. In fact, in this polemic, the figure of Ivan the Terrible is only a point of departure for discussing general problems of power and statehood. Therefore this problem has a definite ideological aspect. This is true of both historical works and works of art.

Chapter 2

Who was Ivan the Terrible?

Grigorovich, well aware of the complexity of the problem, could not escape answering an apparently trivial question—who was Ivan the Terrible? While staging the new ballet Grigorovich had to give an answer *of his own* to this question. Who was Ivan the Terrible for him, a choreographer of contemporary ballet theatre, an artist of the 20th century working in the refined art far from everyday life and scholarly analysis? Grigorovich had to express his own point of view on the character of Ivan the Terrible, taking into account the nature of ballet art in general and his personal artistic attitude in particular as well as the experience of other art forms. There were numerous works of drama, prose and poetry devoted either to Ivan the Terrible or to his times, Lermontov's poem *The Song of Merchant Kalashnikov*, plays by A. Ostrovsky and A. Tolstoy, historical novels and adventure stories to mention a few. One can find the image of Ivan the Terrible in Russian opera (N. Rimsky-Korsakov) and in fine arts (I. Repin, P. Antokolsky). Thus, the works of art devoted to the subject were rather numerous and their authors followed both certain traditions as well as concepts of their own, though as different as those of historians.

In works of art and literature Ivan the Terrible was shown either as a hero of a philosophical tragedy or a concrete human character. The attitude of artists towards the tsar was strikingly different—from reverent sympathy to indignant protest. The 20th century went on with this topic in both traditional and new arts, primarily in cinema. Among the cinematographic works the most impressive and significant was the previously mentioned film by Eisenstein (though it was not the first one).

What attracted numerous artists working in different arts to Ivan the Terrible and his time? On the one hand, it was the same thing that attracted historians. Artists could not remain indifferent to problems of common concern and therefore they tried to find, with their own means of expression, answers to the problems historians and the general public were interested in. On the other hand, there was something else that attracted the attention of writers and artists but escaped the attention of historians preoccupied mainly with ideological and political aspects of autocratic rule.

The point is that the times of Ivan the Terrible had a strong and rather strange histrionic element. The great ruler himself enthusiastically played on the stage of History the part of a reigning comedian, avid for vivid games and theatrical effects.

The histrionic element was felt in both everyday life and political acts of the tsar. The oprichniks were the personal guard of Ivan the Terrible and looked like janissaries, which imparted a flavor of Oriental despotism to the rule of tsar Ivan IV. Their silvery black costumes were decorated with symbolic attributes—a dog's head and a broom—conveying the idea of blind devotion to the master and readiness to sweep treason and dissidence out of Russia. In Aleksandrova settlement, a well-known royal residence, life was regulated by monasterial rules. Clad in monk's cassocks, the oprichniks attended long, exhausting and frantic church services lead by Ivan the Terrible who played, this time, the part of a humble servant of God. Prayers and services, however, did not prevent tsar Ivan and his entourage from participating in equally frantic feasts which occasionally turned into orgies where Ivan cavorted and danced together with buffoons.

Ivan the Terrible had a strong passion for acting. He adored changing costumes and introduced an element of theatricality into political receptions and business meetings. In his paradoxical abdications he enthusiastically played the part of a hurt and haunted man whom no one understood. He worked out a plan of disseminating false rumors about the situation in the country and his own intentions.

Fake conspiracies and treasons, feigned diseases and false omens were all in the arsenal of means Ivan the Terrible resorted to in his struggle for absolute power.

Were there any real conspiracies against Ivan the Terrible? Certainly there were. Were the boyars betraying him? Certainly they were. Serious scholars, however, do not see in such cases any of the phantasmagoric elements Ivan the Terrible was inclined to see. His contemporaries saw him as either a religious fanatic or a jeering jester.

M. Bakhtin, an outstanding Soviet critic and philosopher, wrote that in the times of Ivan the Terrible the uniting and calling toll of church bells oc-

The choreographer wanted to create a Russian national character in Ivan the Terrible. It was important for Grigorovich as Ivan IV expressed the Russian national spirit of that time and he had laid the foundation of Russian statehood. This resulted in the need to represent tsar Ivan in general terms nearly as a character from mythology. As the figure of Ivan the Terrible was taken from concrete historical and political reality of the 16th century, Grigorovich looked for the features which revealed in a way the inner life of Russians.

Although Grigorovich did not neglect the social position of the tsar, he placed him into a broader historical context. And that defined the main line of the development, as he associated Ivan the Terrible with Dostoyevsky's characters. On the other hand, the choreographer wanted to show the tsar from a European point of view as a villain of the late Renaissance and the times of the Shakespearean theatre. This demonstrated Grigorovich's deep historical understanding of 16th century Russia.

At that time the country experienced a number of reforms typical of the Renaissance, though in a specific and limited way. Grigorovich thoroughly studied this period in the history of Russia in order to find an appropriate style and atmosphere for his new ballet and to formulate his attitude to Ivan the Terrible. "I wanted to see my ballet free from both embellished, operatically pompous representation, and simplified, rough and vulgar interpretation of Ivan the Terrible's times," recalls Grigorovich. "Russia of the 16th century was certainly a backward state, but it had already set on a path of cultural and spiritual renewal, leaving behind its medieval backwardness. Russia was going through a definite social upsurge. Its national consciousness was awakening."

It was with this conception of the past that the choreographer staged his new ballet. A ballet with numerous colorful, festive, dynamic and spectacular scenes. A production where even sombre episodes are infused with bright poetic histrionics and the ardor of high passions.

"To portray Ivan the Terrible as an inveterate villain and to make the ballet an instrument of exposing it, is boring," said Grigorovich. At the same time the choreographer saw perfectly well that there was nothing idyllic in the figure of the tsar.

"It is not appropriate to pose a question of whether Ivan the Terrible is a positive or a negative character. Any bias approach is out of place here. It is the scale of this personality that matters. For me, it was important to show a character that the audience would not simply denounce or sympathize with. I wanted people to understand his inner life. Ivan the Terrible may rouse both sympathy and repulsion simultaneously. Good and evil are intricately entwined in him," defined Grigorovich. Besides, he believed that a ballet could not be focused just upon a character totally devoid of any positive element. "A ballet about a villain, villain by nature, is boring," repeatedly insisted Grigorovich. "It is important to show the psychology of the character, to find an answer to the question of what made him remorseless and deprived of any sense of mercy."

Thus, Grigorovich tried to reveal the psychology and inner life of Ivan the Terrible and to define the social and moral idea of the production—a tragedy of power, a dramatic conflict between man and his mission. Ivan the Terrible was preoccupied with his struggle for power and he became enslaved by this struggle. Grigorovich shows that power destroys the human nature of the person who possesses it.

At the time when Grigorovich was staging *Ivan the Terrible* he faced a number of organizational problems. He had to rebuild the Bolshoi Ballet; it was necessary to renew the repertoire and the style, and to undertake decisive measures, breaking away from old concepts and notions, in order to unite the traditions of Moscow and Leningrad schools. It required time for Grigorovich to clearly define his artistic goal and to find a way to attain it.

Work at the libretto. The film by Eisenstein.

It was quite a problem for Grigorovich to find any written material which could serve as the basis for the libretto of his new ballet about Ivan the Terrible. Thus, the choreographer had to write his own libretto that relied upon historical sources. Eisenstein's film was also helpful. Grigorovich borrowed from it some lines of the plot. For example, the secret love of prince Kurbsky for Anastasia. It should be mentioned here that Eisenstein wanted this part to be played by the famous ballerina Galina Ulanova. Grigorovich was aware of this fact that brought ballet theatre closer to the theme of Ivan the Terrible. Grigorovich followed Eisenstein in emphasizing the part of Anastasia in his ballet.

The influence of the film is also felt in the style of the ballet, especially in the scenes which find parallels with the episodes of the film accompanied by Prokofiev's music, for instance, in the scene of the feast of the oprichniks.

Meanwhile the choreographer searched for an original way of tackling the theme of Ivan the Terrible. He had another message to communicate to the audience. He did not share the view point that the tsar's cruelty could be justified by certain needs of the state. Eisenstein followed artistic clichés of his time, which did not suit the choreographer.

Historical sources

Out of a great number of historical works on Ivan the Terrible and his times, Grigorovich paid special attention to *History of the Russian State* by D. Karamzin, which was one of the earliest.

Karamzin was one of the outstanding figures in Russian culture of the late 18th and early 19th centuries. As a sentimentalist-writer, he made a great contribution to the original Russian prose. Romantic elements could also be found in his works. He influenced many Russian poets and writers— A. Pushkin for one. *History of the Russian State* was a work in many volumes. It was the first scholarly work on Russia's past.

Karamzin considered Ivan the Terrible from a somewhat idealistic and romantic point of view. He shared the ideology of Enlightenment which proclaimed that man by his nature was pure and virtuous. From this point of view, the morality of tsar Ivan was distorted in the course of his life and activity. The historian explained the cruelty of tsar Ivan IV by some "bad features" of his character, which strengthened and developed under the negative influences of the environment and circumstances, i.e., Karamzin was of the opinion that though Ivan the Terrible was not a man of gentle disposition, he could not be called a villain either. This point of view was shared for a long time by many Russian historians and publicists. Thus, the outstanding Russian literary critic and democrat V. Belinsky called Ivan the Terrible "a fallen angel."

Karamzin romantically opposed the figure of the tsar to his environment. He apparently took for granted the statements of the tsar though it was well-known that the tsar had interpreted rather freely historical events and facts from his own life. Historians of today know that Ivan the Terrible personally gave instructions to re-write or introduce alterations into the chronicles which were the main historical documents of those times. He changed the chronicles out of political or personal considerations. In his statements and letters tsar Ivan frequently invented things with a purpose to prepare, substantiate or justify some of his measures. Prince Kurbsky, the political opponent of the tsar, used to accuse him of lies and refused to believe some of the fantastic stories of tsar Ivan. For example, the stories, though moving but hardly true, about the unhappy childhood when the young tsar badly suffered from the intrigues of the boyars. The tsar resorted to such stories to justify his hatred for and repressions of aristocratic families. The poisoning of Anastasia by envious boyars was, most probably, another made-up story. "If they hadn't poisoned my young wife, Russia wouldn't have lived to see the rule of Cronos," complained Ivan the Terrible. In such a way he tried to present his evil doings as a retaliative measure. Certainly, poisoning was not an unusual thing in those times, but historians have not found so far any proof of the story. The only witness in this case is Ivan the Terrible himself, and the version of poisoning suited his interests perfectly well.

Karamzin believed the testimony and statements of the tsar. Taking for granted the fact that Anastasia had been poisoned, he attached great importance to it and considered the death of Ivan's wife to be a turning point in his life. He divided the life of the tsar into two periods—prior to the death and after it. The first period was, according to Karamzin, a time of success, reasonable state reforms, glorious victories and rather mild internal policy. The death of Anastasia ruined the personality of the tsar and badly affected his physical condition and his morality. It roused evil forces in his soul. The second period was a time of merciless repression, economic crisis and military defeats.

It is difficult to say today what part the death of Anastasia played in the life of Ivan the Terrible, but Karamzin was quite right when he divided it into two periods. The first one indeed was more optimistic and inspired some hopes while the second one was overshadowed by notorious oprichnina and its consequences. Karamzin, however, exaggerated the importance of personal motivations and factors when he tried to explain complex social processes solely on their basis.

Grigorovich shared the ideas of Karamzin and his understanding of the personality of Ivan the Terrible. Karamzin's version laid emphasis on the personal, emotional and psychological elements in the life of Ivan the Terrible. This approach was, in the opinion of Grigorovich, in line with the nature of ballet theatre. Grigorovich also studied later historical works on Ivan the Terrible. Nevertheless he took Karamzin's version as the basis for the libretto and limited the action to the first period in the life of the tsar. The death of Anastasia was to be a culminating point. That made the line of romance more dramatic which was very important for a ballet production.

While staging the ballet, Grigorovich was in close contact with V. Zimin, a well-known historian and expert on the period of Ivan the Terrible. The choreographer thought it necessary to check whether his understanding of the past did not contradict the contemporary points of view on the subject. On the whole, however, Grigorovich staged the ballet following Karamzin's approach. He tried to incorporate the ballet into the context of Russian culture. By the way, it should be mentioned that Pushkin's historical drama *Boris Godunov* was also based on *History of the Russian State* by Karamzin.

Chapter 3
Secrets of Dramaturgy

How to make a ballet action clear to the audience without a detailed libretto explaining the plot? It was one of Grigorovich's concerns while he was working on the dramatic line of the ballet. He thought it necessary to reconsider the existing methods of constructing the action of ballet productions. The choreographer rejected the idea of consequent story-telling. He split the action into separate apparently unrelated scenes. Each of them had its own complete plot with culmination point, scenes like "Ivan's Disease" or "Battle with Foreign Invaders." Therefore, the libretto only indicated the general lines of the plot without narrating small details of the action. In his approach, the emphasis was laid on how this or that scene revealed the idea of the ballet. Narration was of less importance. Grigorovich was looking for flexibility of the plot. It would allow him to construct the action without any resemblance to literature. Scenes in the ballet depicted some major events in the life of Ivan the Terrible.

It was not the main concern of the choreographer to have direct lines in the plot. Thus, for example, the scenes of the accession to the throne, bride-show and subsequent duet of Ivan the Terrible and Anastasia and Prince Kurbsky's monologue were followed by a battle scene, where the tsar appeared on the battlefield. Everything that had taken place in between was eliminated.

Choreographers advocating the ballet-drama trend would never agree to such a development of the plot. They would insist on showing first the beginning of the invasion and the departure of the tsar to the battlefield. Most probably they would introduce new characters like swordbearers, retainers and heralds bringing the news of the invasion. The solo of Anastasia longing for her husband which in Grigorovich's production follows the scene of the victory over the enemy would seem absurd to them. According to their point of view this scene should rather precede the scene of battle thus making the development of the plot logical.

In *Ivan the Terrible* Grigorovich succeeded in breaking away literary conceptions of constructing the dramatic line which was a distinctive feature of the existing full-length ballet productions. It was the emotional and psychological changes of the characters that created the action. The action emerges from music as such and it was arranged as a free musical composition which evoked various associations. *Ivan the Terrible* by Yuri Grigorovich was a work searching for a new approach rather than a traditional ballet with a plot.

Separate scenes, however, had to be united in a way. But the linking elements should not be part of the action. They rather were to convey some idea and create a theatrical image. For a long time Grigorovich could not find a proper solution. Finally he made his choice—it was six bell-ringers who appear on the stage in between the scenes throughout the ballet. The very times of Ivan the Terrible prompted this solution to Grigorovich.

The point was that bell-ringers had an important social function in Old Russia. It went beyond the limits of their church duties connected with religious rites and rituals.

Church bells were rung on holidays and in times of trouble. The bells warned the people about the approaching enemy and fires. The bells convened people when it was necessary to inform them of important state bills. People were baptized and buried to the toll of church bells.

Old Russian towns and cities were proud of their belfries and bell-ringers. Bell-casters enjoyed esteem among the townsfolk. The secrets of their craft were passed from generation to generation, and Russian principalities competed for getting the best bell-casters.

Like bell-casters, bell-ringers were mainly of humble origin. Their occupation required of them extraordinary physical strength and special skills. Bell-ringers were musicians of a kind since they composed and performed grand bell symphonies. Though the names of Russian bell-ringers did not go down into history people considered them to be genuine artists.

In the times of Ivan the Terrible, bell-ringing was a highly elaborate form of art. The figure of a bell-ringer was a sort of image of that time. Grigorovich conceived the idea to use bell-ringers as a link uniting separate scenes of the ballet. Their dance was to create a special flavor of that epoch. Meanwhile, with the bell-ringers Grigorovich introduced an image of Russian people to broaden the scope of the production and make it more than a personal tragedy.

The Score

At the beginning it was supposed that the score for the new ballet would be made by N. Stassevich to whom the idea of the project belonged. But the plans had to be changed due to his death. Grigorovich went on with the project in cooperation with M. Chulaki, a composer.

While the choreographer was working at the libretto searching for a real dramatic line, he realized that the oratorio did not provide enough musical material for a full-length ballet production. In the course of studies of the historical materials, Grigorovich came to understand that the oratorio did not fully satisfy his conception. Thus, for example, the choreographer doubted whether he needed the oratorio's vocal and choral pieces. He wanted his production to be nothing but genuine ballet. Still the vocal and choral pieces of the score were most attractive. For their melody and emotional expressiveness they belonged to Prokofiev's best. And they had to be kept by all means but not such as written by the composer. They needed quite a new symphonic quality. In other words, the vocal pieces had to be transposed into orchestral ones.

The duration of the oratorio's parts was also a problem. In fact these parts were composed for the film and thus they had their own specific features. A ballet production needed more extended symphonic pieces which gave the choreographer an opportunity to stage large-scale dance compositions. Therefore they had to be extended in time and further elaborated on the basis of the existing musical material.

All that necessitated the creation of a new score for the ballet. It had to be an integral musical composition based on the choreographer's distinct dramatic concept and symphonic development.

M. Chulaki, a close friend of Prokofiev and a well-known expert on his music, took up this most challenging task.

Grigorovich and Chulaki had long known each other. Chulaki had been the manager of the Bolshoi Theatre for quite a long time. He had personally engaged Grigorovich as the artistic director of the ballet company. From his earliest experiences at the Bolshoi, Grigorovich had enjoyed Chulaki's full support. The composer was a great admirer of the choreographer's talent. So when the two of them teamed up for the new work, they were not just partners but artists who had profound understanding and respect for each other. That helped the work at the score of *Ivan the Terrible* to be done in an atmosphere of artistic creativity and research.

Chulaki had to make the score for the ballet in the way Prokofiev himself might have done it. The score included both the oratorio and other of his works. The choice of them was not easy. Out of the composer's heritage he had to select the works which were of the same style and character as the oratorio and correspond to the choreographer's concept of the ballet. Thus integrated in the score were two parts from a rarely performed Prokofiev's Third Symphony based on the music of the opera *The Fire Angel*. The Symphony was written at about the same time as the music for the film. Besides, *The Fire Angel* was composed after the novel of the Russian symbolist V. Brusov. It was a medieval legend and therefore its style had much in common with the story of Ivan IV.

The score also incorporated fragments of Prokofiev's music to Eisenstein's other historical film *Alexander Nevsky* as well as a number of instrumental compositions including *The Russian Overture*.

Chulaki's work at the score was not an easy one. He composed both the "links" between the scenes and new pieces based on Prokofiev's unfinished musical themes. No doubt the latter was of greatest difficulty for Chulaki. He had to compose and integrate new music into the score in such a way that the audience would accept the ballet as a whole.

Chulaki succeeded in overcoming the difficulties. Even experts could not tell the difference between the pieces composed by Prokofiev himself and those written by Chulaki "a la Prokofiev." He produced a unique work. It was a valuable contribution to world ballet art which acquired a masterpiece written by an understanding composer of the 20th century.

Realization of the Concept

During the early rehearsal period Grigorovich often said that in the ballet *Ivan the Terrible* there had to be very little dancing. Of course, he meant "dancing" in the traditional sense of the word. Although Grigorovich had the intention to use the technique of the classical ballet, he was very much concerned with the idea of overcoming its conventional and abstract character. At the first stage of the rehearsals the choreographer was looking for such movements and body expression which would also reflect the historical and national character of dancing.

At the beginning, Grigorovich staged a number of separate scenes of the future ballet. When they were ready he decided to show them to his colleagues, friends, and critics. This was very atypical of Grigorovich who had always tried to avoid presentation of unfinished work to the audience. However, in this case the psychological situation was such that Grigorovich had to test himself. I happened to be among those who saw this unusual presentation. It was obvious that its success became a powerful impulse for the choreographer, who by that time had been working on *Ivan the Terrible* for four years. After the presentation, scholars and critics highly evaluated the work they had just seen. Of special significance for Grigorovich was G. Ulanova's positive assessment of his work.

After the presentation the work at the production entered the second and decisive period. There was just another year of work before the première.

Working with designer

The choreographer's collaboration with the designer S. Virsaladze started just after he had chosen Prokofiev's oratorio and the theme of Ivan the Terrible for his new ballet. The work at the libretto went parallel to the quest for an adequate design. In fact the two processes were organically tied in.

Virsaladze, who had been Grigorovich's permanent partner, came up with a highly effective and expressive design that was not only in line with the choreographer's general conception but further developed and specified it.

The stage accommodated three hinged semicircular constructions reminiscent of church naves or medieval towers. Hence, reproducing the austere spirit of the epoch, the sets provided for continuous changing of scenes throughout the performance. After the end of each scene the characters were veiled by one of the stage constructions while another one opened to introduce the characters of the next scene.

The painted back-drop imitating an ancient Russian fresco was coupled with the overhanging belfry-line of bells with loosely drooping ropes. The rear stage platform accommodating either Ivan's throne or Anastasia's imaginary coffin or the imaginary bride-bed moved up and down the stage.

Costumes were also a problem. They had to respond to a number of the choreographer's and dancers' specific demands: they had to be light, unrestrictive of movements and graphically expressive. Traditional abstract ballet costumes were unsuitable, for the designer intended to convey the style of the epoch and to feature the national traits of the 16th century dress. That is precisely where the problem arose. The 16th century garments were too heavy, fluffy and abounded in adornments. The boyars wore fur coats and their wives had dresses made of very thick materials. People of Old Russia looked like medieval knights in this kind of clothing which restricted the movements.

Therefore Virsaladze was looking for light fabric which could create an effect of heaviness and pomposity. The designer's solution was brilliant. He used an ordinary net as a frame for the traditional ballet tunics thus giving the image of the 16th century garments. In accordance with the choreographer's conception Virsaladze searched for a design which would give a genuine historical and poetic image. He did not want to make a picture of the epoch but rather to convey its spirit.

Chapter 4
Performance

Enthronement.

At the beginning of the ballet six bell-ringers dressed in scarlet-red shirts appear on the stage. They summon people for announcing important news. In the ballet the bell-ringers are always holding the bell ropes. Their first dance is fierce and extremely dynamic. Their movements require high technique of the performers. The dance gives the feeling of the impending tragedy. The crowd which appears introduces the atmosphere of anxious expectation. Then the choreographer presents the envious boyars whose silhouettes are lit up through transparent side naves until the constructions turn about, and the boyars, both men and women, commence their dance.

In the first scene Grigorovich exposes two principal historical forces of the 16th century Russia: boyars and ordinary people. Both groups are anxious about the changes in the country that follow Ivan IV's enthronement. From the very beginning the boyars are presented as arrogant and strutting characters. In the ballet the boyars are the major opposition confronting Ivan the Terrible.

The central nave opens at the moment of general disarray, showing Ivan sitting on a high throne, his head bent low, his hands on the elbow-rests of the throne. He stands up and walks around the throne, suspicious and watchful. The second part of his monologue is performed amidst the quieted boyars and immobile crowd. Ivan's dance consists of high and virtuoso revoltades. He is keeping his hands over his head as if he is holding the crown. There is a call for unity, a striving for absolute power in his monologue. At the end Ivan climbs up to the throne which is the symbol of his absolute power. He casts a victorious glance at Russia which seems spread at the foot of his throne. And the next moment from behind the wing girls start dancing on points to the tune of Russian folk music. The enthronement scene develops into the bride-show; one of the girls is to be chosen the Queen of Russia.

Anastasia is within the group but at first she is not singled out from the corps-de-ballet. The bride-show scene was borrowed by Grigorovich from historical sources. In his first marriage Ivan IV followed the Byzantine tradition: girls from all the boyar families, regardless of the rank, took part in the bride-show. As a result of this democratic procedure Ivan IV chose Anastasia Zakharina. She was not from the highest nobility that caused broad opposition among the elite of boyars.

In the ballet the boyars are also against Ivan's choice. In this scene the choreographer introduces Prince Kurbsky. He is very negative to the tsar's decision.

The girls, the boyars and the crowd disappear leaving Ivan alone with Anastasia. The long romantic duet reveals their feelings. At the end of the scene Ivan and Anastasia ascend the stairs leading to the throne; that also gives the image of the royal palace. The central nave turns around and Kurbsky appears on the empty stage. His monologue completes the initial part of the dramatic line and makes the main conflict evident.

In Grigorovich's interpretation Kurbsky is a brilliant and recherché knight suffering the torments of wounded pride. His dance is full of despair, hatred and loneliness. Kurbsky is consumed with envy of Ivan and seems to be cursing his reign.

Battle

The bell-ringers are back on the stage. This time they are clad in black. They ring about danger, about the invasion of the enemy. The tense and tragic chiming of the bells calls for defense against the invaders. Girls with black shawls, lamenting brides, wives and mothers appear on the stage. Anxiously they are peering into the distance. At this moment all the three naves open to reveal the whole space of the Bolshoi stage. It becomes a battlefield. The bell-ringers and the girls exit. The corps-de-ballet perform the scene of the invasion.

The battle scene is based on a real historical event. At the time of Ivan the Terrible the battle of Kazan became a landmark as it put an end to the Tatar yoke and provided Russia with access to the Volga River and the Caspian Sea. Ivan IV proclaimed the battle of Kazan a sacred religious war called to consolidate the positions of Christianity and demonstrate the might of the united Russian State. In one of his speeches he referred to Moscow as the Third Rome destined to last for ages.

The battle scene is one of the most intensive and spectacular in the ballet. It is performed exclusively by means of dancing. The symphonic music leads the action.

The enemies are presented in a grotesque manner. The line of their dance is broken, they move in small steps on crooked legs set widely apart. In contrast, Russians dance in a free and daring manner. One group of the corps-de-ballet is led by Kurbsky. From history he is known to have displayed great courage during the battle of Kazan. And in the battle scene of the ballet he is also shown as a bold and fearless warrior. His virtuoso diagonal jumps call up the image of a charging sword.

Ivan takes part in the battle too. In fact the battle is presented as if seen through his eyes. To emphasize this Grigorovich introduces medieval allegories—images of death and heralds of victory. The images of death are integrated into the general composition of the battle scene. The sinister figures rush between the lines of soldiers as symbols of bloodshed ruled by death. The appearance of Ivan announces the victory.

The action is transferred to the palace of Ivan the Terrible. Anastasia is in the spotlight. Her monologue completes the second part of the dramatic line.

Ivan's disease

Now the bell-ringers enter the stage dressed in white shirts. They act like buffoons. The bell-ropes dance joyfully in their hands. The stage is brightly lit giving the image of a popular feast. The women are greeting the soldiers who returned victoriously from the battlefield. The mass dance scene symbolizes the triumph of Russia. It is the culmination of the happy period of Ivan's life. The coming future is more dramatic. But now Ivan is still close to his people. His duet with Anastasia is a part of the popular feast, it is rich with folk motifs. In the second act of the ballet Ivan's dance will be gradually losing its national features.

The feast goes on but at the culminating point the lights fade. Some tragic overtones appear in music. The corps-de-ballet comes front stage and falls on its knees. Ivan's throne is lit up in the centre. We see him convulsively clutch his staff. The tsar is ill.

This is a historical fact. During the early years of his reign Ivan the Terrible had some very serious disease. He himself believed his days were numbered. But by some miracle the tsar recovered. Boyars' intrigues while his disease was running its course were a bitter experience for him as they were plotting against the tsar and his heir. Grigorovich introduced this fact into the story to reveal the major conflict between the tsar and the boyars.

In the scene of the disease Ivan is shown alone with Anastasia. She takes care of Ivan who has nearly collapsed. She calls for help and sends prayers to the heavens. But no one is going to help them and they feel lonely; the huge palace is empty and cold. Behind the side naves one can see groups of boyars in dim light: they are waiting for the tsar's death. And no sooner has Anastasia led dying Ivan away from the stage then the groups of boyars become alive. The orgy of pretenders for the throne breaks out. The dancing boyars look like vultures hateful of each other and striving to snatch what they can. Clutching at each other they are crawling up to the throne. Finally one of them manages to push the others away and ascend the throne. But the impostor has no time to rejoice: two hands emerge from behind the throne and seize his throat. Slowly Ivan appears holding his victim. Horrified, the boyars crawl away. Their eyes are fixed on Ivan who strangles the impostor. The dead body rolls down the stairs. The tsar throws his staff across the stage and it sticks in the floor amidst the kneeling boyars. This is the last scene of Act One.

Poisoning of Anastasia

Act Two opens with a love duet of Anastasia and Ivan. The choreographer has called this duet "Ivan's happiness." Meanwhile the duet is a sort of prologue to the tragic culmination of the ballet. At the end of the adagio the lovers are set in each other's arms. The light picks up the boyars who are watching the idyll. After the lovers disappear behind the central nave the boyars stealthily fill the stage and start furiously circling it. All of a sudden the boyar women appear carrying a massive golden goblet. At first everybody starts back from it in fear. Yet the idea of poisoning has already been planted into the minds of boyars. The goblet is being slowly passed around. Everyone touches it timidly and swiftly passes it on to the neighbor, apparently not daring to become an executor. At the height of the ritual dance with the goblet Kurbsky rushes in. The boyars hide the goblet but then they let Kurbsky into the plot. Kurbsky is confused, but he sees no way out. He cannot accept Anastasia's death, yet he is overwhelmed by envy of Ivan. The boyars give him the goblet. They persist in pushing him to the crime. Finally Kurbsky desperately grabs the goblet and rushes to the platform on which Anastasia suddenly appears. She takes the goblet with poison. Pause. Kurbsky makes an attempt to stop Anastasia, but it's too late . . . Grigorovich creates a very strong mise-en-scene: Anastasia is standing on a tall platform, the goblet in her hand; the descending line of the boyars departs from it like a poisonous train.

The monologue of dying Anastasia is one of the most moving scenes of the ballet. The main idea becomes evident. The struggle for power, the clash of political interests kill someone who is absolutely innocent. It is even more tragic when this person is a beautiful woman. Political intrigues and struggle for the throne are immoral and can not be justified. Thus, both the boyars and Ivan the Terrible are responsible for Anastasia's death. This message borrowed from the legendary story of the poisoning communicates a profound social and philosophic meaning to the ballet. The choreographer suggests the idea that personal happiness is incompatible with the struggle for power.

The movements of Anastasia's last dance are very simple yet utterly expressive. She seems to be just melting away and departs from life with quiet obedience. At the end of Anastasia's last monologue the boyars leave the stage and only Kurbsky stays. He tries to reach her but the central nave turns and Anastasia disappears forever.

Sedition

After the scene of Anastasia's death the bell-ringers reappear on stage, dressed in black mourning shirts. Their fierce dancing mirrors the commotion of the people. The uprising is about to break out. The corps-de-ballet rushes around the stage. Clenched fists are shaking at the blank walls of the imaginary towers. A short scene of the sedition opens the central line of events of Act Two. The outrageous masses seem to urge Ivan to take drastic measures.

It is known from history that in Old Russia every important event happening in the royal family provoked an immediate reaction of the people. Ivan the Terrible, the tsar of Russia, was largely recognized by the popular masses. On the contrary, ordinary people disfavored boyars whose selfish policy harming the masses resulted in numerous conflicts. Ivan IV was well aware of this fact. A wise politician, he took advantage of the situation, encouraged people to oppose boyars and declared the latter guilty of all the troubles in the state. The terror against boyars was much supported by popular masses who wanted to see Ivan as their protector against the despotism of the aristocracy.

Ivan at Anastasia's coffin

Ivan's dance at Anastasia's coffin is his most significant solo in the ballet. This solo turns into a fantastic scene in which the ghost of the poisoned wife appears to Ivan the Terrible. This scene is the most emotional and passionate in the production.

The solo is set on an empty stage. The choreographer introduces acrobatic elements into Ivan the Terrible's movements and brings them into harmony with the movements of the classical dance. Ivan is overwhelmed with a variety of feelings: one moment he is filled with sorrow, the next one he is wildly desperate, then he flies into a violent rage. The solo is created in such a way that the tsar seems to be drawn to the earth: grief and suffering never allow him to straighten up, they literally bend him in a physical sense. The dance here contains many parterre positions and bent-knee postures suggesting the image of a prayer for the repose of the dead soul. Just once or twice this pattern of dance is broken by flying virtuoso pas as if expressing the character's resistance and his attempts to overcome the tragedy. The idea of Ivan's solitude reaches its peak in this scene.

Exhausted and half-mad, Ivan lies prone on the stage. This is when the central nave begins to shine in a most mysterious way. Girls appear in the moonlight just like angels descended from the heavens. Candles are burning and a children's church choir sounds quiet and ethereal. The nave turns and opens the platform which now resembles a tombstone. The ghost of Anastasia comes out of the group of girls. Ivan approaches the ghost. Anastasia bends over him and hangs poised with her head down behind his back. The impressive cross-shaped lift symbolizes the burden of Ivan's sufferings. He moves towards the center with his hands stretched out to the sides. The adagio of Ivan the Terrible with dead Anastasia resembles the images of Old Russian icon-painting. The ghost of Anastasia seems to drift over Ivan bemoaning their common tragedy and at the same time consoling him. In the culmination of the adagio the cross-shaped lift is repeated again. Anastasia, surrounded by the angels-girls, disappears when Ivan reaches the platform-coffin. The lights fade.

Kurbsky's flight

The short scene of Kurbsky's flight anticipates the scene of oprichnina. Kurbsky flies across the empty stage in a dance imitating the wild galloping of a horse. For Grigorovich the reason for Kurbsky's flight is motivated by fear of the tsar, Anastasia's death and most of all by horror of what he has done. As compared with history Kurbsky in the ballet is greatly romanticized. In reality he was not in love with Anastasia and did not poison her. The actual reasons for Kurbsky's flight were much more trivial than those shown in the ballet. But as an artist, Grigorovich was free to suggest a completely new image of Kurbsky. For Grigorovich, Kurbsky symbolized human weakness that under certain circumstances can lead a man to treason or crime. At the same time Kurbsky is shown as a human being who might arouse sympathy and understanding. Kurbsky, like the tsar, is also lonely. He is a stranger to both Ivan and boyars. He is equally repulsed by both the tsar with his claim for absolute power and by the boyars with their plots and intrigues. Kurbsky is lost in the stormy and controversial world. Thus, his flight is inevitable.

Grigorovich introduces the groups of boyars conjured by Kurbsky's imagination into the scene of the flight. The boyars come on the stage from the side naves holding goblets which strikingly resemble the one given to Anastasia. The corps-de-ballet of the boyars is accompanied by the symbolic figures of death already familiar to the audience from the battle scene. The boyars are carried away by them. Kurbsky's dance again gives an impression of a galloping horse. The stage becomes empty and dark. One can hear a solemn choral tune, peaceful and devout. Human figures wrapped in long gowns with hoods appear on the stage. Glittering candles in their hands fill the stage with a faint deceptive light. The flow of people keeps growing as it moves slowly towards the black platform in the central nave. Standing on the platform is Ivan leaning on his staff, dressed entirely in black and resembling a pilgrim monk.

Oprichnina

The scene of oprichnina begins with a prayer. People with candles in their hands kneel humbly before the platform which symbolizes an altar. Ivan blesses them and crosses himself in a solemn and grave manner. But then the prayer quite unexpectedly changes its character. A whip appears in Ivan's hand and the quiet and pious ceremony is interrupted by its lashes which are strengthened by imperative beats of the staff. The black figures respond to these sounds. They straighten up and begin moving to the rhythm set by Ivan. Another moment, and all the hoods are down; the gowns thrown open and reveal silver chainmail underneath. These people are oprichniks, each of them is holding a whip just like Ivan's.

The wild dance of the oprichniks creates the impression of fanatic and cruel power. In an ominous round dance with axes, ropes and banners they are ready to crush everything. Ivan leads this bacchanalia which gradually becomes extremely violent. The oprichniks drag the boyars onto the stage with ropes around their necks. The boyars cross themselves in fear crying for mercy. Three buffoons scurrying about the stage among the boyars and oprichniks enhance the general phantasmagoric atmosphere of action. All of a sudden the fourth buffoon, dressed differently from his three fellows appears on the platform. His face is covered with an ugly mask, his gown is silver-black and he holds a goblet above his head. The boyars, guarded by the oprichniks, stand stockstill. The buffoon holds out the goblet to everybody and then, stepping down from the platform, offers the boyars to try the contents. No one accepts. Finally he gets tired of the show and snatches a rope from one of the oprichniks. The other end of it appears to be tied to a boyar. The boyar attempts to run away but the buffoon manages to step on the rope and the boyar falls. The buffoon slowly pulls the boyar towards him and stretches out the goblet to him. The boyar refuses. But the buffoon forces him to drink. The boyar writhes in the agony of death. The mysterious buffoon disappears from the stage to reappear a bit later with a knotted stick in his hand, a grotesque imitation of Ivan the Terrible's staff. Suddenly he throws back his head, slowly takes off his mask and the buffoon's gown. It is the tsar. One of the oprichniks gives him his real staff. Ivan the Terrible turns to the boyars surrounded by the oprichniks. At the tsar's sign the oprichniks begin to herd them together holding axes over their heads. Ivan the Terrible, his sceptre high in the air, makes his way towards the group, ready to strike the enemies with his own hand. Suddenly he makes an abrupt turn and thrusts his sceptre into the ground. The central nave turns to cover the oprichniks and the boyars.

Finale

The ballet ends with Ivan the Terrible's monologue. It expresses tragic desperation and finishes with a passionate appeal for national unity. Here Ivan is terrible as known from history. He is imbued with a frantic thirst for power symbolized by the golden royal sceptre. His dance in this scene seems to reveal a variety of his most controversial feelings and emotions.

Flame-robed angels appear in Ivan's imagination. The girls in scarlet tunics with long swords in their hands encircle Ivan. The world in Ivan's mind turns red and the stage is gradually flooded with red light. Just as at the beginning of the performance bell-ringers dressed in red shirts appear on the stage. The platform moves forward. Ivan the Terrible mounts the platform and tries to catch the bell-ropes and put them together. At last he tightly holds them in his hand. The bell-ringers below on the stage pull the ends of the ropes in different directions. The platform begins to move backward. The ground is slipping away from under Ivan's feet. He throws his legs over the ropes and hangs in the air, himself like a bell.

Première. Dancers.

The première of the ballet *Ivan the Terrible* was a tremendous success. For 11 years now it has been in the repertoire of the Bolshoi Ballet. It is most frequently performed by the company. It has also been a great success on all the major tours in the U.S.A., England, France and other countries.

During the 1976–77 season Grigorovich staged the same version of the ballet at the Grand Opera in Paris where it was also a great success. Starring were: Jean Guizerix (Ivan) and Dominique Khalfouni (Anastasia).

The first cast in Moscow included Yuri Vladimirov (Ivan), Natalia Bessmertnova (Anastasia) and Boris Akimov (Kurbsky). The choice in many respects was quite unexpected but right.

Of medium height, sturdy and with a sportsman's figure, Vladimirov did not look in the least like Ivan the Terrible. But still Grigorovich saw his exceptional dramatic gift that broke the traditional scenic image of the legendary tsar. Vladimirov succeeded in performing the grotesque and eccentric parts of the role. But what was more important he managed to get into Ivan's psychology, to show the emotional and impulsive inner world of the tsar. With his passionate temperament Vladimirov revealed the whimsical and capricious nature of his character and the sudden contrasting changes of his emotions. The dancer was especially persuasive in the scene where Ivan is on the verge of madness, tortured by violent and conflicting passions.

Boris Akimov was rather young at the time of the première. He had an excellent technique. But for a long time there was no appropriate role for him. In *Spartacus* he was Crassus in the second cast. In *Swan Lake* he danced the part of Rothbart. But his type was that of a romantic character and thus he was brilliant in the part of Prince Kurbsky. He managed to create a poetic image of a person imbued with melancholy and sadness and at the same time to show his courageous and energetic features. These latter were vividly displayed in the scene of the battle. Still the leit-motif of the character is that of his hopeless love for Anastasia.

The main parts in the ballet were also performed by other leading young dancers. For example, Mikhail Lavrovsky and Vladimir Vasiliev, a well-known master whose interpretation was psychologically more refined, and later the most brilliant soloist of the present-day company Irek Mukhamedov, danced the part of Ivan. Both experienced Mikhail Gabovich and young talented Andris Liepa appear today in the part of Kurbsky. Among the outstanding ballerinas in the role of Anastasia one can see Lyudmila Semenyaka who has superb technique and high artistry.

Natalya Bessmertnova as Anastasia was magnificent. She had all the necessary qualities both as an actress and as a ballerina to depict the character of Ivan's wife. Her individual icon-like style was in harmony with the general conception of movement and scenery in the production. Bessmertnova's metaphoric dance, far from the details of everyday life, was in line with the choreographer's idea of the symbolic image of Anastasia. Bessmertnova's dance revealed a real Russian character which seemed to come from Russian legends and traditions.

Yuri Grigorovich with his wife Natalya Bessmertnova—the star of the Bolshoi Ballet.

Synopsis

In the gloomy times of the Middle Ages the Tsar Ivan IV ascends the Russian throne. Boyars, who represent Russia's nobility of the highest rank, strongly oppose the supreme power of the new Tsar. Among them is Prince Kurbsky. He was one of the main contenders to the throne and he is filled with hatred for his lucky rival.

According to an old Russian tradition the Tsar must choose a wife for himself from the most renowned boyar families. Ivan IV makes his choice. It is Anastasia who fascinates the Tsar with her delicate beauty and graciousness. Boyars are fuming with rage and indignation, as Anastasia does not belong among the boyar elite. Prince Kurbsky who was secretly in love with her is shattered by the news of her proposed marriage to the Tsar. Not only did Ivan strip him of power, but he also stole his beloved. Kurbsky is consumed with insane jealousy.

The internal conflicts and intrigues are forgotten for the time being in the face of a great national danger. Russia is being threatened with an attack by the Tatar hordes. For centuries Tatar invaders had been raiding the country, robbing people, burning towns and villages, killing and raping . . . Tsar Ivan calls for his people to repulse the hateful enemy and do away with the barbarians' yoke once and for all. Left alone in the Palace, Anastasia prays for Ivan. A bloody battle between Tatars and the Russian warriors ends in an absolute victory for Russia.

People joyfully celebrate their triumph and glorify the victorious Tsar, the protector of Russia. At the height of the celebration Ivan is suddenly overtaken by a mysterious disease. His days are numbered and the boyars begin competing for the throne behind his back. Thinking the Tsar must already be dead, one of the boyars succeeds in ascending the throne. But Ivan together with Anastasia manages to overpower death. Miraculously, he recovers.

In the midst of the boyars' intrigues against him Ivan emerges from behind the throne and strangles the impostor with his own bare hands. The boyars retreat in awe.

Ivan and Anastasia enjoy their happiness. But the boyars never cease plotting against them. Being too cowardly for an open riot they decide to poison Anastasia, knowing she is the apple of the Tsar's eye. They persuade Prince Kurbsky to avenge himself on his enemy Ivan. Blinded with hate and envy, he agrees. Anastasia feels she is in danger but she cannot believe it may come from Kurbsky. Unsuspecting she accepts a goblet of poison from his hands. Having recovered from the spell of rage for Ivan, Kurbsky bitterly repents, but it is too late . . . Anastasia dies. The only thing he can do now is flee.

Ivan is overwhelmed with grief. The thought of Anastasia's death is unbearable to him. Ivan is haunted by the visions of his late beloved and their irretrievable happiness. At her coffin he swears to avenge her. There is no undoing the injustice, but it must be requited. Bloody and horrible will be Ivan's revenge. Ivan summons an army of "oprichniks"—fanatics, ruthless and cruel, ready to follow whatever terrifying order he chooses to give them. They always keep their eyes open for the slightest sign of treason. They do not hesitate to torture and kill. Masqueraded in a buffoon's costume Ivan himself takes part in the torture of the boyars. Awful is the retribution for Anastasia's murder. Ivan's oprichniks destroy everything and everybody whom they suspect of disloyalty.

Thus Ivan, called by the people " the Terrible," becomes an absolute ruler of Russia, his ominous power infinite and formidable.

In old Russia the bell-ringers were the first to bring any piece of news, be it good or bad . . .

. . . The bells toll solemnly, summoning the young and the old to hear an announcement of primary importance—the enthronement of a new tsar.

The Tsar is sitting proudly on his throne ominously surveying his subordinates. From now on everything is in his power: the fate of the whole country and every human life in it.

boyars, Russia's nobility next in rank only to royalty, are all apprehensive of the new monarch. They detest the thought of his power over them. Ambitious as they are, the boyars are consumed with envy and hatred.

The boyars, members of the most distinguished families of Russia, are confused and seized with fear in the face of a new supreme power. Each of them may have had his own aspirations to the throne.

Prince Kurbsky is fuming with indignation. He was one of the main contenders to the throne. He cannot reconcile himself to the idea of his defeat . . . and he does not hide his feelings.

Tsar Ivan IV, who would later be called by the people "The Terrible," is celebrating his triumph. His hands are over his head as if he were holding a crown—the eternal symbol of absolute autocratic power.

According to an old Russian tradition a "bride-show" begins. Young girls from all the boyar families, regardless of their rank, appear before the tsar. One beauty after another passes before the throne, but it is only Anastasia who fascinates the tsar with her refined beauty and graciousness.

The tsar makes his choice despite the fact that Anastasia does not belong among the boyar elite. Like the rest of the highest nobility, Prince Kurbsky is indignant at the Tsar's choice, though for his own reasons ...

Ivan is charmed by Anastasia's delicate beauty, her tenderness and sincere innocence. A scarf in her hands is a symbol of her maidenhood.

Anastasia begins to respond timidly to Ivan's feelings for her. The lyrical duet of Anastasia and Ivan develops into a passionate and fiery dance of love.

Prince Kurbsky, who was secretly in love with Anastasia, is shattered by the news of her marriage to the tsar.

Not only did Ivan strip Kurbsky of power, but he also stole his beloved. Prince Kurbsky is consumed with jealousy and filled with hatred for the new monarch.

The bells are ringing an alarm. People spill out onto the square. The chiming of the bells calls for the defense of the country against foreign invaders. Lamenting wives, brides and mothers anxiously peer into the distance after the departing warriors.

For centuries Russia suffered from frequent Tatar raids. The barbarian invaders are threatening the motherland with another attack. They present grotesque figures, their curving scimitars gleaming ominously in sinister moonlight.

The Tatar invaders are confronted by the regiments of Russian soldiers. Carrying the banners of saints as a symbol of Christianity against the pagans, they'd rather die than suffer defeat.

Russian and Tatar warriors cross their weapons in a severe battle. One after another they fall to the ground. The image of Death reigns over the battlefield.

Prince Kurbsky is one of the real heroes of the battle. A truly courageous warrior, he inspires others by his heroic example.

Tsar Ivan calls on his regiments for the last deci-sive blow to the enemy. He is really "terrifying" in battle.

Ivan delights in fighting. Daring and fearless, he leads his warriors against the monstrous Tatar hordes. His sword is raised high in the air proclaiming victory.

Anastasia, left alone in the palace, is overcome with anxiety for her husband, her imagination drawing terrifying pictures of the bloodshed he is engaged in. Sad is her dance, imbued with a longing for her beloved.

Anastasia's lyrical reminiscences alternate with outbursts of despair. She tries to push away the frightening thoughts in the hope that her great love will protect Ivan from deadly danger.

Happy is the reunion of the tsar Ivan and Anastasia after his victorious return.

Ivan is overwhelmed with love and tenderness for his wife. In utter abandon Anastasia trustfully clings to him. Her happiness is boundless.

Anastasia's coterie of girls joins the exulted lovers to glorify their love and fidelity. There is nothing to fear as long as they are together.

People are feasting to celebrate Russia's total victory over the barbarian invaders. They joyfully greet valiant soldiers and glorify the victorious tsar in a mass dance of triumph.

At the height of the celebration Ivan is suddenly seized with a mysterious illness. Anastasia never leaves his side, her coterie of girls praying to God not to let Ivan die.

In vain does Anastasia call for help. There is no one to hear her desperate cries. She and Ivan are deserted by all their subordinates in the face of the coming tragedy.

Ivan is desperately struggling against his disease and Anastasia is the only one to support and comfort him. Terrifying visions pass before the sick tsar's eyes.

The boyars weave intrigues waiting impatiently for the tsar to die. Stealthily they watch his sufferings. Every one of them aspires to the throne, feeling that the tsar's days are numbered. Miraculously Ivan recovers . . .

The boyars never anticipated the tsar's recovery. Exultantly they clutch at each other in an attempt to reach the throne.

Finally one of the boyars manages to ascend the throne. Unexpectedly Ivan emerges from behind the throne. He ruthlessly strangles the impostor with his own bare hands.

The boyars retreat in awe. Terrible is the tsar in his rage. The strangled boyar lies at his feet while he suspiciously surveys his subordinates trying to spot treachery.

Ivan and Anastasia are together again. The nightmare of Ivan's ailment is all in the past. The boyars' riot is suppressed. Nothing seems to cloud their happiness any longer.

Ivan's love for the tender and sweet Anastasia is the joy of his life. Ruthless as he is, he grows kinder and softer at her side. She is God's blessing to him.

Ivan realizes that Anastasia is his guardian angel and he thanks Heaven for the happiness granted to him. However, not long will be the days of their blissful idyll.

The boyars are plotting against the tsar. Being too cowardly for an open riot, they plan to avenge themselves on the monarch by poisoning his beloved wife. A goblet is sinisterly passed around from hand to hand.

One of the boyars pours poison into the goblet. Everyone stiffens in tense expectation. The boyars persuade Prince Kurbsky to cast a fatal blow to his enemy Ivan. Despite his deep aversion to the thought of Anastasia's death, yet suffering the torments of wounded pride and blind with hatred, he agrees.

Anastasia is in fear of the evil forces surrounding her. Yet, unable to suspect Kurbsky of such an atrocity, she accepts from his hands the villainous gift of the boyars and swallows the poison.

Anastasia blindly wanders round the palace. Kurbsky follows her trying to plead with her for forgiveness. But she cannot any longer hear him. She is overtaken by death.

Prince Kurbsky cannot stand
to see Anastasia's death.
Having recovered from the fit
of blind rage for Ivan he is
tormented with repentance.
But it is too late. Nothing can
be done to save Anastasia's
life.

In a final attempt to overpower death, Anastasia calls upon her last reserves of strength. As if by magic, she seems to have overcome evil powers. But it is an illusory impression. That is an agony, the precursor of death.

The last moments of Anastasia's life are imbued with pain and suffering. For her there remains an unspoken question of why such a brutal injustice has been done to her . . .

Unconscious, Anastasia collapses into Prince Kurbsky's arms. Though in terror of the tsar, the boyars feel victorious. Their perfidious plan has been enacted.

The boyars exult in their triumph. They do not suspect that death and terror are in store for them. Frightfully cruel will be Ivan's revenge for the murder of Anastasia.

Distressed and furious, Ivan curses his enemies and swears to avenge Anastasia. Rage and despair, grief and a thirst for blood, all these contradictory feelings tear at his heart. At night he comes to the church to be close to Anastasia's dead body. There is no way to undo the injustice, but it must be requited.

Great is the tsar's sorrow. He is driven half-mad with grief. At Anastasia's coffin Ivan pours out his heartache. The misfortune that befell him drains him of all strength. In his visions he sees Anastasia alive again.

As in the scene of the "Removal from the Cross" Anastasia droops in Ivan's arms, while he vainly tries to relive the memory of the past happy days.

The ghost of his murdered wife soars over Ivan. He seems to be hearing the voices from Heaven reminding him of the by-gone moments of joy and happiness.

New people appear in Ivan's retinue. They are called oprichniks. The tsar summoned them to avenge himself on the hateful boyars. The boyars are doomed. Bloody massacre and violent reprisals would be their fate. The lashes in the hands of oprichniks symbolize the coming retribution that no one will be able to escape.

Ivan directs the oprichniks himself. And they follow him servilely with dog-like obedience.

Ivan calls on the oprichniks to have no mercy for boyars—the traitors—to spare no one.

Hatchets fly up in the hands of the oprichniks over the boyars' heads.

The tsar himself takes part in the massacre. Having changed into a buffoon's costume in order not to be recognized he mocks and tortures his victims.

Oprichniks herd the boyars to the place of execution. Proud and inexorable stands Ivan holding a gold scepter which symbolizes his absolute power.

Swords soaked in boyars' blood are outstretched in the hands of the oprichniks—the "angels" of revenge. The bells toll with increased power. Ivan the Terrible addresses his people with a passionate appeal for national unity under his guiding reign.

His glance fierce and ominous, Ivan the Terrible proclaims his infinite formidable power over the land and the people . . .

Conclusion

The ballet *Ivan the Terrible* opened a new period in Grigorovich's artistic career. Since its première the choreographer has staged such great productions as *Angara, Romeo and Juliet, The Golden Age, Raymonda*, etc. A new generation of dancers achieved its top level in his ballet.

Ivan the Terrible asserts Grigorovich's artistic principles and his understanding of ballet as theatrical art that includes music, dance and painting. This is an art of clear and distinct dramatic conception, an art which communicates its ideas to the audience with its large-scale expressive means.

Z-105
IVAN THE TERRIBLE